T0114757

ON THE
Edge
OF LIFE

A TRUE STORY OF
FAITHFULNESS

Paula Citron Averitt

WESTBOW
PRESS®
A DIVISION OF THOMAS NELSON
& ZONDERVAN

WestBow Press books may be ordered through
booksellers or by contacting:

WestBow Press
A Division of Thomas Nelson & Zondervan
1663 Liberty Drive
Bloomington, IN 47403
www.westbowpress.com
844-714-3454

ISBN: 978-1-6642-8862-1 (sc)
ISBN: 978-1-6642-8861-4 (e)

Print information available on the last page.

WestBow Press rev. date: 3/20/2023

CONTENTS

PREFACE

I'm glad you are reading this book and I pray that God uses its contents in your life, just as He did mine as I was writing it. Nothing that God does through a person's life is wasted; it is always used for His greater purpose. I wrote this book expressly how I sensed God leading me, so some of the chapters are shorter than others. It is mainly written for you Christ followers and, specifically, you who are going through a difficult time in your life. Those who don't know Christ may also glean from this book what a relationship with the Lord looks like and how we live. My desire is simply to get a clear and impactful message across. May it bless you deeply.

Paula Citron Averitt

"Worthy are you, our Lord and God, to receive glory and honor and power, for you created all things, and by your will they existed and were created." Revelation 4:11 ESV

ACKNOWLEDGEMENTS

First and foremost, I want to thank you, my Father and Lord, Jesus Christ, for allowing me to be used by You as You do Your work in and through my life. There are no words to express the gratitude I have for your faithfulness and love toward me.

I would also like to thank my loving husband, Steve, who so graciously listened as I read each chapter as I wrote them, and my three wonderful friends who edited my book; Connie Averitt Williams, Michael M. Moses and Debbie Ostrander. I am forever grateful for your input and insights.

CHAPTER 1

❖

A Lesson in Grace

"And of his fullness we have all received grace for grace."
John 1:16 KJV

Hello. So, I was sitting here, at the end of the day, January 2, 2019, reading yet another book, and the thought came to mind, "Write your own book." Write my own book? I thought. As I walked downstairs to get my laptop, I sensed that it was His idea (God's that is).

It all started that night, when I was watching what seemed to be an endless number of contestants on The Voice or Britain's Got Talent and everyone had these beautiful voices, one after the other. It really was astonishing to listen to. That led me to watching YouTube videos of songs that were coming to mind. All these people putting their lives out there and, at some point, I just started thinking..." I need to write a book about my life." MY LIFE? Now what would that contain?? Should I start with my marriage to Steve?

Of course, so much has happened in my life before Steve and I came together... but I somehow think this isn't even about that. It's not really about the circumstances IN my life, it's about MY LIFE! Who I am.... And part of that is the fact that I am penning this right now. As I started writing, I got the impression, this was somehow God's way of rebuilding me. Not long ago, I was sensitive to and recognized that I was on the "Potter's wheel"... and remembered that one week before, I realized that I am clay. It's true. He is the Potter and we are the clay. Amazing, really, how fragile we are – but when the pot is not looking the way the Potter wants it to, He just rebuilds it. There are no words for this. How amazing is it that God will just tear down and rebuild His masterpiece? He knows what He is doing.

So, right now, as I am writing, I am sensing this has something to do with water. We need water, in more ways than one. Physically, we need water to live and spiritually, we need water to live... *"...the water I give them will become in them a spring of water welling up to eternal life."* John 4:14 NIV. We were dead in our trespasses when Jesus came to earth and He is this life-giving water. Thank you, God, for water…your water.

It all started when Steve and I were in a Sunday school class together, many years ago. We were dating at the time (2009) and as he participated, this sense of competition came over me. Let me be absolutely clear, life is not about competing with anyone. God sees us all, equally, as His children and we are all owned by Him. The church is about uniting us into one as we use our gifts for the edification of one another. There's no room for competition here…. That's a worldly trait and has no place in the Kingdom of God.

It was as if I forgot we were on the same team and thought that he was somehow ahead of me and I was falling behind. I'm not sure why I felt that way, maybe because I didn't know Steve very well, what his spiritual gifts were…?? Which now I know are exhortation and teaching. Or maybe it was something else…?? I saw that he was progressing and it made me look at myself. Hmm… maybe that's what it is…?? I started comparing…Which is another dangerous trap. In any case, this is what started a distorted view of life for me. I was with a man, whom I married, and didn't have the right view of him or myself.

So, how is God changing that? Well, first, I must admit that I had been a bit resistant to the change God wanted to do in my life. Then I got to the point where I just cried out to Him, "Change me!!!", as if it were the last words I would ever speak. I meant it, and I suddenly heard something inside me say, "God given desires." Yes, that's what I want in my life, God given desires. And not just that, I want Him to help me express to Him all that I have been holding back in my life. There is something deep within us that just wants to cry out to God with all that we have to move us, change us and help us. If you are a Christ follower, you will know how important this is. But beyond that, what I am finding is, it is even more important to talk with God. I mean really talk to Him. Not in a quick way where you gloss over things. I mean really pour your heart out to Him. He is waiting and wanting to hear from His children.

Things have happened in my life that I wish never happened; ways that I have neglected others, tried to control things and said that I didn't want to do what God wanted me to do…He has a deeper purpose and a plan for the things that happen in our lives. And might I say that He is using it to make us better?!?! It really doesn't feel that way sometimes, but it's true. He is making us more like Him, every day. That is His plan, and that is His way… Shaping us and molding us, to become more like Him.

So, what does He do with those things we have so terribly messed up? Am I out of this mess yet?? He uses it to glorify Himself. He is faithful and will always work things out for our good, our sanctification, which brings Him glory. God is good and He will never fail us. Deuteronomy 31:8 ESV says, *"It is the LORD who goes before you. He will be with you; he will not leave you or forsake you. Do not fear or be dismayed."*

We sometimes think that we can get away from God, but that's not true. Psalm 139:7-10 NIV says: *"Where can I go from your Spirit? Where can I flee from your presence? If I go up to the heavens, you are there, if I make my bed in the depths, you are there. If I rise on the wings of the dawn, if I settle on the far side of the sea, even there your hand will guide me, your right hand will hold me fast."*

Do you want to know something?

After suffering an acute form of mental illness, I personally experienced trying to run away so far that I actually felt something like a boundary that I could not cross. However hard I tried to cross it, I could not. This was NOT my moment of glory. This was my mistake.

I was saved at the age of eight and fully turned my life over to Christ when I was thirty-six. In the first few weeks and months of that relationship I was riveted to see what the next thirty years would be like!!! I had never known this love and fellowship before. It was all I had ever wanted in my life and, as a part of this, I poured my life into my husband (at the time) for three years and he ended up divorcing me because of my faith. This was heartbreaking. I wanted nothing more than for him to see what he could have, who he could be, who he was in Christ!!!

Even more heartbreaking was that I thought God had let me down. He had promised that all my household would be saved. Acts 16:31 NIV says, *"… Believe in the Lord Jesus and you will be saved – you and your household."* …and I believed it with my whole heart. I believed God's word to me, but from this vantage point, it just seemed that that wasn't going to happen; At least not through me. It was hard to make any sense out of it, and all I knew was that everything was falling apart.

But God knew it all. He knew my pain, my suffering,

my lack of understanding. He knew where I would go, and for how long and why I even went there (to that boundary I couldn't cross). Sometimes we can do things that don't even make sense to us. It just doesn't seem like something we would do. But He was there. The whole entire time and He's here now. He just never gives up on us. He is making us a new creation.

Over time, things began to change. Life became more "normal." My mind started working better. Things were just more clear. I was making better decisions and I could pray. I had started asking God for more of life. More of Him. He answers prayers like that! He wants us to know Him fully. And He is so worth knowing!! Nothing compares to Him. This is called Grace. Grace is God's way of showing us not only who He is, but what He has done that covers all the mistakes we will ever make. This is His Story. It's all about Him…And I lay myself down, for my whole life is in His hands.

I have been wanting to say this for some time now and I'm glad I am finally getting it out. Praise God for prayer and for His purposes in our life. He truly knows best and it's in our best interest to rest in knowing that. He is truly larger than life and nothing can compare with Him. He is our great companion, our Friend, our Father, our heart, our Lord, our peace, our strength, our wisdom, our hope, our joy, our everything! He is the one who sanctifies and we praise Him for that. There is hope in knowing this.

How He deals with us is personal…We all have different lives. Nevertheless, He is our Father and will always be there for us and with us. We are forgiven, by His grace.

_____

_____

_____

_____

_____

_____

_____

_____

_____

_____

_____

_____

_____

_____

_____

_____

_____

_____

CHAPTER 2

Letting Him In

*"Therefore, since Christ suffered in his body, arm yourselves
also, with the same attitude, because whoever suffers in
the body is done with sin. As a result, they do not live
the rest of their earthly lives for evil human desires, but
rather for the will of God."* 1 Peter 4:1-2 NIV

S eeking to know God is pretty spectacular. One of the things high on the list is learning to let Him in. There are quiet times and there are some not so quiet times. It is liberating, nonetheless. He wants to help us work this out…Every day, every hour – and He is great at it!

So, what are some reasons you don't want to let Him in? Are you afraid He is not going to approve of what you are doing, thinking or saying? Is it that He has high expectations? His motives are pure…and He is working to bring you into the light.

He wants honesty. Is that really so hard? How can you be honest with Him today? He knows you love Him and He cares for you. Honesty is all about telling Him the truth. No matter what it is, He can handle it. You are not going to break Him down. He just wants to hear it from you. Nothing that you say is going to turn Him away. He WANTS you!

Now, I've thought about this for a long time. There have been so many things in my life that I haven't wanted to look at. Things that make me feel like I'm not worthy. I went to bed on this, but when I woke up the next morning and my husband left for work, I started thinking… "Do well." The first thing that came to mind was, okay… I've been hurt by some people in my life and I found quickly that I was ready to move on from that. Later, I found myself thinking about the hurt again, and the emotion around it seemed to come back on me like glue.

So, I'm realizing that I really have to watch my thoughts. Have you ever watched what you were thinking? It reminds me of the passage in 2 Cor 10:5 NIV that says, *"…and we take captive every thought to make it obedient to Christ."* God gives us this ability. It requires your focus and it's worth it. Why? Because we will no longer be trapped by the vagueness that seems to plague us when we are not filtering those thoughts and making sure only the right ones are being accepted.

When something comes to your mind, you must determine if it is of God or not – because thoughts can also come from you, the world, and the enemy, and a discerning mind will not allow anything that is not of God to take root in it. You must be resolute about this. This is what it means to have the mind of Christ.

Now, let's talk about prayer. We know that prayer is our way of communicating with God. Talking with Him, asking Him for things we need, praying for others… Is this line of communication open? If not, how do you open it? I would start by thanking God for His resources. There is nothing that He withholds from His children and His resources are endless!

Wow! Now THAT'S something to think about! This will give you faith. Faith in His abundance! He is not lacking anything and He doesn't want you to lack anything either. So, the more we thank God for, the more faith we will have in Him. The key here is to be specific. What else can you thank God for? Do you appreciate Him? Tell Him!

I thank you, Lord, for your grace, thank you for your infinite mercy, thank you for your faithfulness, thank you for your presence, thank you for your loving kindness, thank you for your compassion, thank you for saving me, thank you for loving me, thank you for hearing me, thank you for knowing me, thank you for prayer, thank you for teaching me, thank you for pursuing me, thank you for who you are, thank you for what you are doing in my life, thank you for what you are going to do, thank you, thank you, thank you!!!

When you are going through something hard, it is even more important to thank God, so you don't lose sight of Him. *"Give thanks in all circumstances, for this is God's will for you in Christ Jesus."* 1 Thes 5:18 NIV. In doing this, we are lifting Him up – exalting God over everything else in our lives. This is what makes life so precious. *"And as Moses lifted up the serpent in the wilderness, so must the Son of Man be lifted up, that whoever believes in him may have eternal life.* John 3:14-15 ESV.

One of the things I want you to remember is that we NEED Him! We absolutely NEED Him. I have needs, you have needs, we all have needs...and Jesus is there, waiting for us to ask. Remember, He is the God of abundance! All we have to do is ask.

_____

_____

_____

_____

_____

_____

_____

_____

_____

_____

_____

_____

_____

_____

_____

_____

_____

_____

CHAPTER 3

Being Obedient

"If you love me, you will keep my commandments"
John 14:15 ESV

So, now that we've talked about God's grace and letting Him in. I want you to ask yourself, what do I think of when I hear, "Be obedient." What does that sound like to you? Is it hard, like someone is shaking a stick at you? Does it sound like someone is forcing something on you? Or are you in a place where you are gratefully accepting it (obedience) and want to do it. What does it look like to you? For me, I will say I am willing. I want to follow God and do what He says, and I hope you do too. When we are obedient to God, we are saying, "Yes, Lord" and "I love you, Lord."

Now, there is a difference between the choices God gives us and a command. Are you listening?? What I mean is, are you listening to Him? We first must be paying attention if we are going to hear what He wants to say to us. So, the first thing we ought to be doing is listening. Has God told you to do something?

For me, it is a few things. I know I heard Him tell me very directly to learn a new language. I also sensed Him giving me the idea and gently moving me with His hands to write this book. He also wants me to "wait" for Him in prayer and study His Word. I know what He is asking of me right now. Do you? God speaks directly to us and as we read His Word, He will show us what His will is for us as we "hear" His commands. *"Do not merely listen to the word, and so deceive yourselves, do what it says."* James 1:22 NIV.

Before we go any further, I want to go back to your prayer life for a minute. This is the most important part of your journey. Talking with God and asking Him for what you need. Aren't you thankful that we can go to God in prayer?? What_a blessing that is to us all. Today, I found myself asking_for wisdom. There are things we need and we just can't do without them. Asking God for these things helps us to get where we are going. Please tell me you are on this journey with me. If you feel you are lacking anything, will you ask God to fill that need? Asking God for help is a sign of submission. It is saying to God that we need Him.

_____

_____

_____

_____

_____

_____

_____

_____

_____

_____

_____

_____

_____

_____

_____

_____

_____

_____

Praising Him

"Praise the LORD, all nations! Extol him, all peoples!
For great is his steadfast love toward us, and the faithfulness
of the LORD endures forever. Praise the LORD!"
Psalm 117:1-2 ESV

As I finished writing the previous chapter, I felt the need to stop and praise God. He is so kind and worthy of our praise. I often wonder, why would He care to love one such as me? He is so giving and worthy of honor, praise and worship. We belong to Him and He is ours. Loving hearts adore Him. We will be in communion with Him as we lift Him up.

Have you thought about praising God? What that really is? It's giving Him your heart. It's saying "Thank you for who You are and what You have done." Has He changed your life??? YES! And is He continuing to work in your life??? YES! Has He come alongside you at times in your life??? YES! Is He faithful to complete everything He has promised??? YES!!!

One of my many favorite verses is Philippians 1:6 NIV – *"Being confident of this, that He who began a good work in you will carry it on to completion until the day of Christ Jesus."* What an amazing promise! No matter what happens or how things look, He is faithful to finish what He started in you!

Does that mean we are always going to know or understand every little detail? No. God calls us to look to Him and not our circumstances. Please read your Word.

Nothing can give you what you need like God's Word. His promises are true, His Word is clear and we will rise above it all! Praise God for His love.

Did you know that praise is going on in heaven day and night (our day and our night that is)? All day and all night, the heavenly host are praising God. What we do down here should resemble what is going on in heaven.

God has prepared a place for us and we show how grateful we are by praising Him. There are no words to describe the magnitude of what God has done, in His infinite mercy. He is worthy!

How do you show your gratitude by praising God? How do you worship? Think about it.

Paula Citron Averitt

_____

_____

_____

_____

_____

_____

_____

_____

_____

_____

_____

_____

_____

_____

_____

_____

_____

※

CHAPTER 5

Trust... Your Mercies Fail Not

Those who know your name trust in you, for you, LORD,
have never forsaken those who seek you.
Psalm 9:10 NIV

If there is one thing I must talk about, it is trust. Life has
been hard for me at times and I am just now coming
back to a place of trust. God is willing to help us get
back there if for some reason we are finding it hard to
trust Him.

I remember hearing a word come to me while in
Sunday school when there seemed to be a lot of talking
going on and confusion about what was being discussed.
The word was specifically, "Trust God." It gave me the

deep understanding that God is in control and I didn't have to be concerned. This is the opposite of trying to take control of things. How do I know that? Because I've done that!

God wants us to trust Him with our lives…and He can be trusted at ALL times. Not just sometimes, but ALL times. Why? Because He knows what is best and He is never wrong. Have you ever trusted God like that? Letting go of all the things you are holding onto and letting Him direct your path…guide your life??

Choosing to let Him have what is rightfully His… You! He purchased you with His blood and you belong to Him.

So, what does trusting God look like? …Day to day, walking it out, I mean…

As I write this, a lady whose daughter I had in my Sunday school class several years ago is coming to mind. I have no particular reason to think of her. I haven't seen her in what seems like years. Anyway, why is she coming to my mind? Is God choosing to put her on my mind so I can pray for her? Well, I will, because I believe God is doing just that! Has God put someone on your mind? Do you pray for that person?

What about waiting times? Right now, I believe I am in a waiting time with God. Some might call it God's waiting room. He wills for me to be "waiting" for Him and He has His reasons –ultimately for my good and His glory. I sensed today that He is humbling me. I also sensed that He is preparing me. How He does what He does isn't always clear to me, but one thing I do know and that is He is always at work! Whether I can see it or not. It can be hard to "wait" sometimes. It can also hurt to be molded and shaped into something different. But I will let Him do it because I love Him…. I will trust Him.

What about temptation? Temptation to go and do your own thing and not "wait" … Well, that is certainly something we all can struggle with. But once you recognize it, you can tell God you trust Him. By all means, He created me! Of course, I am going to wait! He knows why I am waiting.

Tell Him you love Him. Everyone wants to hear that they are loved by you… God is no exception. You tell your mom you love her, your dad, siblings, aunts, uncles, grandparents. God too wants to hear that you love Him. Of course! …you are His child.

No matter what is going on in your life right now, you can tell God (your heavenly Father) you love Him… and anything else that might be on your mind.

So, what IS on your mind? I remember taking a walk not long ago and I heard my Lord say to me, "What is on your mind?" There were three things I was thinking of that seemed to be pretty big – I measure that by how much attention I am giving those things. Anyway, I walked through each of them and realized that until that moment in time, I wasn't really talking about them with God. He wants to hear from us. Even if it seems small. He is listening.

I want full-on trust. What does God say about trusting Him? There are many verses in the Bible on trust but I will touch on one command and promise we all know and love:

Proverbs 3:5-6 NIV says, "*Trust in the LORD with all*

your heart and lean not on your own understanding; in all your ways submit to Him and He will make your paths straight."

This passage says to trust in the LORD with all your heart. I want to emphasize the word, "ALL", here. Do you think God wants some of our heart? Nope. He wants ALL of our heart. It takes trusting Him with our whole heart to not lean on our own understanding.

Then it says, in all your ways submit to Him. Again, I want to emphasize the word ALL. In ALL your ways submit to Him. Not some of your ways, ALL of your ways. That means every single thing you do. Turn to Him and ask Him to show you the way.

He is perfect and knows what the right way is for you. Trust Him. Walk with Him.

_____

_____

_____

_____

_____

_____

_____

_____

_____

_____

_____

_____

_____

_____

_____

_____

_____

CHAPTER 6

Presenting Yourself to Him

*"Now to Him who is able to keep you from stumbling,
and to present you faultless before the presence of His
glory with exceeding joy, to God our Savior, who alone
is wise, be glory and majesty, dominion and power, both
now and forever. Amen."* Jude 1:24-25 NKJV

No matter what is happening in your life right now, God already knows it. He knows it! Doesn't that give you confidence in Him? He is aware of all your trouble, and troubling thoughts that seem to have power in your life. Did you get that? ...I said, "seem." I say that because God is our true source of power, through the Holy Spirit. Think about that.

He is waiting for you to come to Him. There is nothing He can't do, but I believe what He wants to do most, is just hold you in His arms and love you. He will rekindle the fire within you, Beloved. He has everything in His hands...it's His Mercy.

It's communion that we are talking about here. Being face to face with Him and heart to heart. Resting in His truth, being forthcoming with our needs, asking Him for help. His lovingkindness will guide us. He cares for us.

Want proof?... Living proof??? Who saved you... <u>YOU or GOD?</u> Who keeps you... YOU or GOD? Who desires you...<u>YOU OR GOD?</u> Okay, that last one was obvious. Well, actually, aren't they ALL obvious? He is not going to make a mistake with you...He is perfectly waiting for you.

You know what makes me think? This awareness that God is "waiting for me." He loves me so much that He wants to be with me, RIGHT NOW! Knowing all the things I know about myself...and He still wants me... That's deeply humbling.

Some time ago I was listening to a sermon on the radio and the pastor said something that I knew I needed to heed. He said, you need to read the Bible for yourself! Don't just listen to what others are saying – Even the pastor of your church. You might go to a service one Sunday and not remember that evening what was said. Know what the Bible says.

Another way we present ourselves to God, is by going to His Word and trusting what He is saying to us. When we do this, we are believing Him and He is honored.

Believing God. Have you ever thought how much that pleases Him? What more can I say about this?

_____

_____

_____

_____

_____

_____

_____

_____

_____

_____

_____

_____

_____

_____

_____

_____

_____

CHAPTER 7

A New Beginning

"In the beginning was the Word, and the Word was with God,
and the Word was God, He was with God in the beginning."
John 1:1-2 NIV

I find it fitting to remember these verses of Scripture when thinking of a new beginning, mainly because our new beginning is always with the Lord himself. It is

Him who we are turning to, it is Him who we are being prepared for, it is Him who desires us to be like Him.

Do you need a new beginning?? I am remembering a time when I was in the hospital because of some mental distress I was experiencing. I didn't want to be there, but that's where I found myself.

At some point in my past, I began to have problems with the synapses in my brain working the way they should. This caused me to go through a number of years, on the edge of life. Not being able to process thoughts the way I should. This was a horrific time for me and to be honest, I just wanted it to end.

But the timing of all this was in God's hands. He knew how long I would be going through this experience and why. And no matter what, He ALWAYS came to me with His Word. The Light of Life. Never a day went by when I didn't see His hand in my life. He was "walking" with me through it. It was hard, don't get me wrong, it was very hard, but knowing that He was there made it endurable.

The promise that God is with us 'til the end is true, and I really didn't understand the full meaning of it until I went through it myself. I was so in need, every single day, every hour, every minute. It took all I had to keep reminding myself of what God had said or showed me.

So, what is He doing now? As I mentioned earlier, He told me to learn a new language (which is Hebrew) and I am writing this book, as the Lord guided me to.

Now, my husband has a cat named Leo, who has been known to be very cantankerous. Over the past five years, since he's been living with me, I've been picking him up every day and showing him that he is loved.

One day, as I picked him up, I sensed God telling me this is temporary. The first thing I thought of was that He was saying the cat is temporary and I need to turn my eyes toward Him, who is Eternal. He wants me to focus on and be comforted by Him.

The second, more poignant thing I thought of, was that the things of this world are going to pass away and I don't want to have my heart and mind set on the things of this world, because I know one day soon, it is all going to disappear. The Bible puts it this way:

"Lift up your eyes to the heavens and look at the earth beneath, for the heavens vanish like smoke, the earth will wear out like a garment, and they who dwell in it will die in like manner; but my salvation will be forever and my righteousness will never be dismayed. Heaven and earth will pass away, but my words will not pass away." Isaiah 51:6-7 ESV

Paula Citron Averitt

_____

_____

_____

_____

_____

_____

_____

_____

_____

_____

_____

_____

_____

_____

_____

_____

CHAPTER 8

A Life on Display

A s I was resting for a while from writing, I came to sense that God was telling me He wants my life on display. Now that can be scary. My life on display??? What does that mean exactly? Who from the Bible can I look at whose life was on display? Well, just about everyone! In the pages of Scripture, we see and hear lives that are crying out to God, praying to God, singing praise to God, running from God, resting in and trusting God and worshipping God. Of course, there's more, and it's all right there, laid out in the pages of God's Word. So, what does that look like for me? Somehow, I know I am about to find out... Your will be done, Lord.

As I was deciding to help a sister in Christ today, I sensed God witnessing to me that I was emptying myself. *"...but emptied Himself, taking the form of a bond-servant..."* Philippians 2:7 ESV. The NIV states it this way, *"...He made Himself nothing by taking the very nature of a servant..."* Philippians 2:3-4 NIV says, *"Do nothing out of selfish ambition or vain conceit. Rather, in humility value others above yourselves, not looking to your own interests but each of you to the interests of others."*

Humility, self-denying, servanthood. Considering others better than yourselves, being concerned with the interests of others. What an amazing and fulfilling way to live; Giving your life to others. What does that look like for you?

I'd like to talk for a while now about garments. Just as we have physical garments that we wear, we also have spiritual garments. Over the past few months or even year, I would say, God has brought this to my mind. It is important for us to acknowledge these garments and wear them.

We are to wear a garment of Praise! *"Through him then let us continually offer up a sacrifice of praise to God, that is, the fruit of lips that acknowledge his name."* Hebrews 13:15 ESV

Colossians 3:12-14 NIV says, *"Therefore, as God's chosen people, holy and dearly loved, clothe yourselves with compassion, kindness, humility, gentleness and patience. Bear with each other and forgive whatever grievances you may have against one another. Forgive as the Lord forgave you. And over all these virtues put on love, which binds them all together in perfect unity."*

Here I am, three chapters later and still "waiting". Do I sound impatient? Maybe I am a little. But I'm learning that too! Patience while God does His work establishes a person's character. The main reason I brought it up again, was to emphasize that there's more to waiting than you might think.

Today, I sensed again that God wanted me to wait for Him in prayer. There's a BIG difference between the "Not doing anything" type of waiting and the waiting where you seek God, trust His judgements and His way of doing things, Praise Him still, love Him still, suffer with Him still.

I have to admit and I already expressed this to God… it hurts! Waiting patiently, while God shapes and molds me into who He wants me to be, sometimes hurts.

He knows best!

Paula Citron Averitt

_____

_____

_____

_____

_____

_____

_____

_____

_____

_____

_____

_____

_____

_____

_____

_____

_____

CHAPTER 9

The Work is Done!

*"How much more, then, will the blood of Christ, who
through the eternal Spirit offered himself unblemished to
God, cleanse our consciences from acts that lead to death,
so that we may serve the living God!"* Heb 9:14 NIV

Of all the things I have learned, in all the time I have
lived and things I have been through, the one thing
I know for sure is the work is done! He has accomplished
everything for us; it is finished and complete. We just
need to trust Him.

Just as He marks the times and the seasons, He also

justifies our lives in Him. By simple submission, we walk in Him and let His life grow in us. He will forever be our God and nothing can change that!

This should give you great peace, my friend. Knowing that God has done for us all that is necessary for salvation, sanctification and glorification. We adore Him and Praise Him. For His life and His life alone is what saves us; not ourselves.

> For now, I see the sun is a shining, for now I see a light to light my way.
>
> I breathe for just a moment, and now old things have passed away.
>
> I will never leave thee nor forsake thee, our Father says to thee.
>
> He will ever be in our presence, loving God, Savior is He.
>
> Light the moon and all the stars, give us hope when days are grey.
>
> Loving Father we adore thee, every night and every day.

Do you know Him like that? Do you know that He is waiting for you to fully surrender to His love?

While in my car seeking the Lord's face, I sensed Him saying to me, "I will take care of you." So, why am I trying to protect myself?? Good point, I said. Do you try to protect yourself? It might help to remember that, *"old things are passed away, behold all things are become new."* 2 Cor 5:17 KJV. The old things are the old ways of life in which you once lived. You don't live there anymore! Your citizenship is in Heaven now and you are owned by the Lord our God, the King of Israel!

"You are the salt of the Earth!" He says, in Matthew 5:13 NIV.

So, what is God asking of you? Is it time to commit to Him? Commit to honor, adore and love Him? Isn't that what a relationship should look like? Honoring, adoring and loving? We are certainly not overlooking obedience here, for obedience is certainly our life's work. We honor God in our obedience, we adore God in our obedience, we love God in our obedience.

Obedience is belief. Belief in what God has said.

He is kind and loving and patient with us, but we cannot forget that where we are going is a place of true faith and trust. Loving Him with our whole heart and knowing that He has our best interest at heart. He will never lead us somewhere He isn't going to use to grow us. Trust Him….He will never fail you. He is fully able to lead you, if you will let Him.

Are you an open door? Are you softening toward Him? I just finished reading the story of Jacob and Laban in Genesis and I see God's omnipotence, protection and goodness on display…. How He opened Leah's womb when Jacob chose Rachel over her and how God told Laban not to say one thing good or bad to Jacob when he set out to find him.

Jacob worked for Laban for 20 years but left Laban

with all his family and livestock because he wasn't being treated right. Jacob realized that Laban's attitude toward him had changed. But God knew it and told Jacob *"Go back to the land of your fathers and to your relatives, and I will be with you."* Genesis 31:3 NIV.

Jacob reminded his wives that he worked for their father with all his strength, yet Laban changed his wages ten times. But God did not allow Laban to harm him. The Scriptures tell us, *"If he said 'The speckled ones will be your wages,' then all the flocks gave birth to speckled young;and if he said, 'The streaked ones will be your wages,' then all the flocks bore streaked young. So God has taken away your father's livestock and has given them to me."* Genesis 31:8-9 NIV

Do you see how God protected and provided for Jacob? God knows how to take care of us. I just feel like worshipping Him right now. Giving Him all the praise and glory for all He is and does and lifting my heart to Him. Do you feel the same way?

He is calling you…Follow Him!

I sensed that my heart is wanting to support missions. Not long ago I heard the word, "harvest" in my heart. Nothing that is ever done for the Lord is wasted or not worth it. He is WORTH IT! His Kingdom is worth it! He has everything in His hands and will bring everything to pass.

If you are not looking to Jesus, what are you looking at? Who are you looking at? What is it that makes you move? What motivates you? Who motivates you and why? There is only one thing I want to ask you today… And that is… Since God made you, why wouldn't you put your affections on Him? Why would you settle for something less? People cannot fill the desire and needs you have, money certainly cannot fill those desires and needs, vacations and sporting events and every other recreational thing you can think of cannot fill the desire and needs you have.

There is a place we call "home", and literally it is just that. That place is found after a conscious decision is made to "come home." To return from whence you came. Return to God. Return to love. Return to the one who created you. This is where your desires and needs are fully met.

Not one will be left unfulfilled.

Paula Citron Averitt

_____

_____

_____

_____

_____

_____

_____

_____

_____

_____

_____

_____

_____

_____

_____

_____

CHAPTER 10

Do What God Has Designed You to Do!

"But you are a chosen race, a royal priesthood, a holy nation, a people for his own possession, that you may proclaim the excellencies of Him who called you out of darkness into his marvelous light." 1 Peter 2:9 ESV

D o you know what God has designed you for? One might think, "He made me to be a teacher," another might say "He made me to be a lawyer" or "doctor" or "plumber." "He designed me to sing", "…be a pastor", "…an administrator."

The moment the title of this last chapter came to me, I realized that it is going to be the weightiest of all the chapters in this book… and rightfully so, because our whole life culminates in this one thing and it runs deep.

The answer to what I asked above is worship. That is what God designed you to do. He designed you to worship Him. So, what does that look like? First of all, we give ourselves to the Risen King, Jesus Christ. We devote our lives to Him, we give our heart to Him, and our very being, for He created us and deserves our all.

Then… expect Him, be quiet before Him (If you are talking about it, you're not doing it). Rely on His Word, rest in Him, surrender. You will never know the love He has for you until you submit to Him. Let Him be the one you turn to, cherish and adore.

I had turned away from finishing this book for a time, and one night, suddenly, I had been "moved" to finish it. I realized at that moment what the last chapter title was going to be because it was my obedience in writing this that made me realize I was worshipping Him through it.

When we are doing the "thing" he called us to do… for example, give our testimony, we are worshipping Him. When we are trusting Him, we are worshipping Him. When we are praying, reading His Word, singing His praises and using the gifts he has given us, we are worshipping Him. It is an act of obedience to worship and His love brings us to this place.

This act of obedience is of the heart. It is with our heart that we love our Lord, that we seek Him night and day, that we desire to be with Him, that we turn toward Him, that we submit to Him and live according to His ways.

"But the hour cometh, and now is, when the true worshippers shall worship the Father in spirit and in truth; for the Father seeketh such to worship him. God is a Spirit: and they that worship him must worship him in spirit and in truth." John 4:24-25 KJV

He knows you.

Have you learned to trust Him yet? Have you asked Him to help you? Are you willing to lay down your life? He lives for us and is waiting for you. Everything is in His hands.

So, I pray this encourages you to let worshipping God be the purpose of your life. He will NEVER disappoint you. I praise God for who He is and all that He is. It is deeply intimate and wonderful living for Him and with Him, fulfilling His desire for me and for others. Only He can know what that will do in people's lives. Praying for many to come to know Him.

> *"And Jesus answered him, It is written, You*
> *shall worship the Lord your God,*
> *and him only shall you serve."* Luke 4:8 ESV

Paula Citron Averitt

In closing, may I leave you with a poem I wrote about
our God?

He knows, who you are,
And He made you, just like the star,
That lights the way
To the place, where Jesus lay.

And He knows, where you are,
And He made the path you trod,
In simpleness, just profess His Great-fullness.

He will come to you,
He will fight for you,
He will always seek you,
and draw you near.

There is none like Him,
In His faithfulness,
He will always see you through.

In your circumstance,
In the darkest night,
He will prove to be your light.

God of all the earth,
God of wonder,
God of Truth,
God of Life.

Printed in the United States
by Baker & Taylor Publisher Services